Penguin Readers

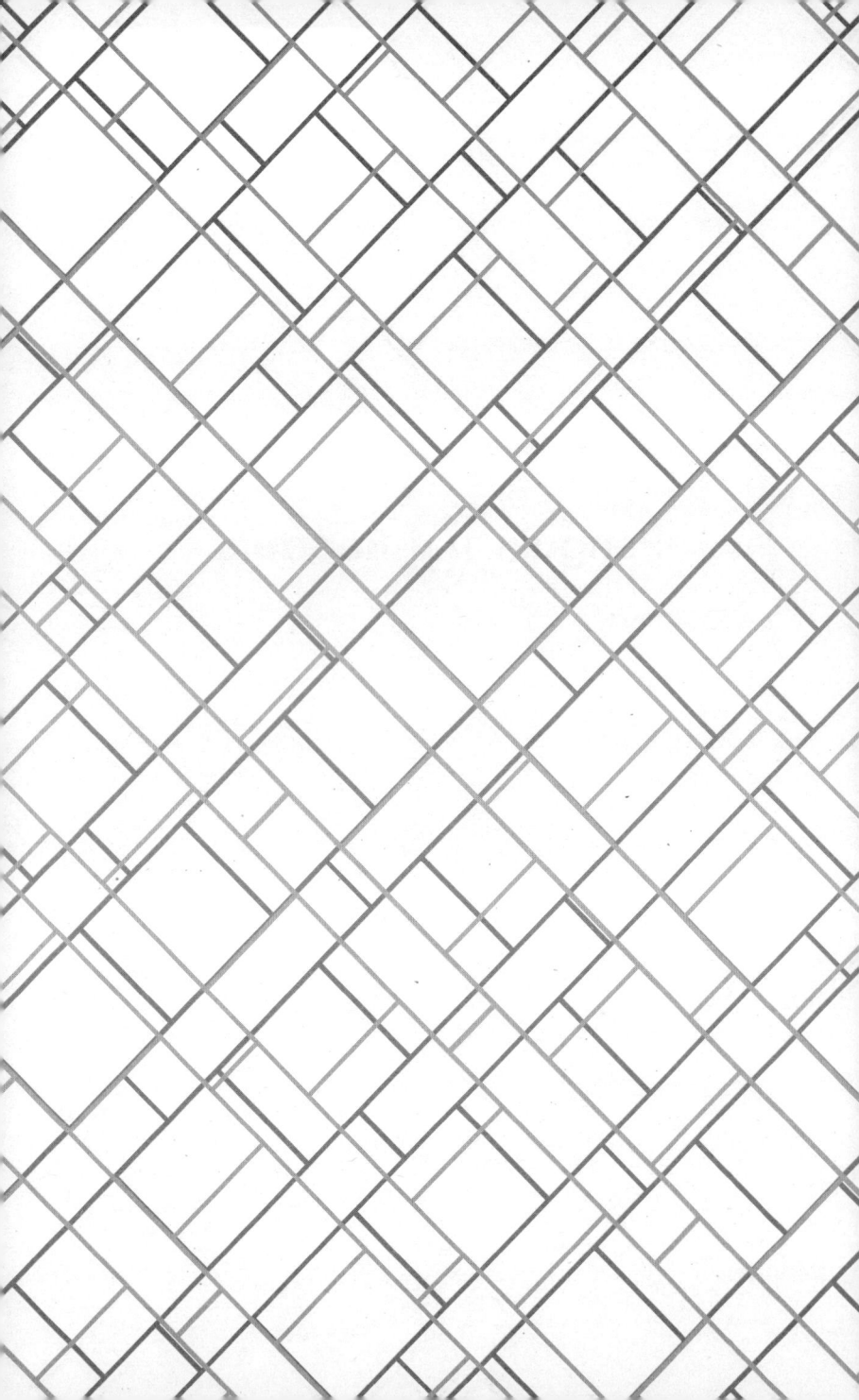

A FESTIVAL IN SUMMER

ANNA TREWIN

LEVEL

ILLUSTRATED BY CHELLIE CARROLL
SERIES EDITOR: SORREL PITTS

GLASTONBURY, GLASTONBURY FESTIVAL and PYRAMID STAGE are proprietary trade marks belonging to Glastonbury Festivals Limited.
This is a work of fiction. Names and characters are the product of the author's imagination and any resemblance to actual persons, living or dead, is entirely coincidental.

PENGUIN BOOKS

UK | USA | Canada | Ireland | Australia
India | New Zealand | South Africa

Penguin Books is part of the Penguin Random House group of companies whose addresses can be found at global.penguinrandomhouse.com.
www.penguin.co.uk www.puffin.co.uk www.ladybird.co.uk

First published 2026
001

Text written by Anna Trewin
Text copyright © Penguin Books Ltd, 2026
Illustrated by Chellie Carroll
Illustrations copyright © Penguin Books Ltd, 2026
Cover illustrated by Shahid Mahmood and Chellie Carroll

Penguin Random House values and supports copyright. Copyright fuels creativity, encourages diverse voices, promotes freedom of expression and supports a vibrant culture. Thank you for purchasing an authorized edition of this book and for respecting intellectual property laws by not reproducing, scanning or distributing any part of it by any means without permission. You are supporting authors and enabling Penguin Random House to continue to publish books for everyone. No part of this book may be used or reproduced in any manner for the purpose of training artificial intelligence technologies or systems. In accordance with Article 4(3) of the DSM Directive 2019/790, Penguin Random House expressly reserves this work from the text and data mining exception.

Printed and bound in Great Britain by Clays Ltd, Elcograf S.p.A.

The authorized representative in the EEA is Penguin Random House Ireland, Morrison Chambers, 32 Nassau Street, Dublin D02 YH68

A CIP catalogue record for this book is available from the British Library

ISBN: 978-0-241-75370-5

All correspondence to:
Penguin Books
Penguin Random House Children's
One Embassy Gardens, 8 Viaduct Gardens,
London SW11 7BW

Penguin Random House is committed to a sustainable future for our business, our readers and our planet. This book is made from Forest Stewardship Council® certified

Contents

People in the story	8
New words	9
Note about the story	10
Before-reading questions	10
Places in the story	11
Chapter One – Tickets for Glastonbury!	13
Chapter Two – First night	18
Chapter Three – Where are Mum and Dad?	24
Chapter Four – Summer Song	34
Chapter Five – On the Pyramid Stage	38
Chapter Six – Back home	50
During-reading questions	54
After-reading questions	55
Exercises	55
Project work	59
Glossary	60

People in the story

Katy and Charlie Mercer

Mr and Mrs Mercer

Adriana Perez

Jo, Pete, Toria and Kenji (Adriana's backing dancers)

New words

artist

food stall

stage

theatre

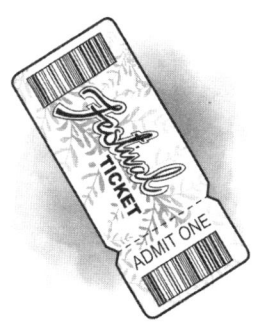
ticket

Note about the story

Glastonbury is a **huge*** music **festival** in England. **Around** 200,000 people go to Glastonbury every year. The festival is usually in June. Many famous music artists play there, but there is also theatre and dance. There are hundreds of food stalls.

The festival is between lots of **hills** and it is very beautiful. There are many stages at Glastonbury. The two big stages are the Other Stage and the Pyramid Stage. The Pyramid Stage is very famous.

Buying tickets for Glastonbury is very difficult because a lot of people want them!

Before-reading questions

1 Do you like music? What music do you like?
2 Read the "Note about the story". When is Glastonbury? What can you see and do there? What are the names of its stages?
3 Look at the map on page 11. Where is Glastonbury? What city is it near?

*Definitions of words in **bold** can be found in the glossary on pages 60–61.

Places in the story

CHAPTER ONE
Tickets for Glastonbury!

It is evening at the Mercers' house in Bristol. Katy Mercer and her brother, Charlie, are watching *Britain's* **Talent Contest** on TV. Mr Mercer is cooking dinner in the kitchen and Mrs Mercer is on her **tablet**.

"What are you doing, Mum?" asks Katy.

"I'm **entering** our names for Glastonbury tickets," says Mrs Mercer.

Charlie **laughs**. "**Thousands** of people enter for those tickets, Mum," he says. "You enter every year, and you never get them."

"I know," says Mum. She laughs too. "But I love trying."

"Look, Charlie," says Katy to her brother. "This dancer is very good. His name's Ezra Smith."

Charlie and Katy watch the dancer. Charlie loves dancing, and Katy loves singing. They always watch *Britain's Talent Contest*.

"Yes, Ezra dances very well," says Charlie. "Maybe he can **win** the contest."

"Look, I got them!" **shouts** Mrs Mercer. "We have tickets for the Glastonbury music **festival**!"

"Wow!" says Charlie. "Well done, Mum!"

"What artists are in the **line-up**?" asks Katy.

Mum reads from her tablet. "We can see the Dusk, Louise Lockwood, Cold Break, Jackie Olson . . . Oh, and Adriana Perez!"

"Adriana Perez!" shout Katy and Charlie together.

"Yes," answers Mum. "She's **headlining** on the Pyramid Stage on Saturday night!"

"That's **wonderful**!" shout Katy and Charlie. "We can see our favourite artist!"

TICKETS FOR GLASTONBURY!

CHAPTER TWO
First night

It is the first day of Glastonbury, and the family are at their **tent**. The festival is between many big green **hills**. It is beautiful here. The family can see the **crowds** and the Pyramid Stage from here. Dad is reading about the festival in his programme.

"There are lots of **areas**!" he says. "There are a hundred stages and hundreds of artists! There are lots of **cafés** and restaurants. There are **quiet** areas and dance areas. There are areas for young children, and there are hospital areas too. There are lots of food stalls. There's food from **around** the world here."

"Did you say food?" asks Mum. "Because I'm hungry. What time is it now?"

"It's six o'clock," says Dad. "Let's find some food and listen to some music."

FIRST NIGHT

A FESTIVAL IN SUMMER

The family walk down the hill into the festival. There are thousands of people here, and they are all talking and smiling. There are families and people from around the world. People are selling **colourful** festival clothes in big tents. There are hundreds of food stalls.

FIRST NIGHT

The family eat some Chinese food. Then, a young woman paints Charlie and Katy's faces.

"I'm a cat!" says Katy.

"And I'm a bird!" says Charlie.

The family walk to the Other Stage and watch Jackie Olson. She is great, and they dance to all her songs. There are lots of colourful lights on the stage. It is wonderful.

"Tomorrow, Adriana Perez is headlining on the Pyramid Stage!" says Charlie to Katy.

"I know!" says Katy. "I'm very **excited**!"

FIRST NIGHT

CHAPTER THREE
Where are Mum and Dad?

It is a beautiful morning. Charlie and Katy are wearing their Adriana Perez T-shirts. It is Saturday, and Adriana is the headlining artist on the Pyramid Stage tonight.

The family make breakfast at their tent, and Dad reads from his programme. "We've got a great line-up. Black and Red Theatre group are at the theatre **field** at one o'clock, and Cold Break are at six o'clock on the Woodsies Stage. We can finish with Adriana Perez at nine o'clock at the Pyramid Stage," he says. "What a great line-up of theatre and music!"

The family eat breakfast, then Mum and Dad sit in the sun. Katy and Charlie play football with children from other tents.

WHERE ARE MUM AND DAD?

At 12 o'clock, the family walk into the festival and **through** the crowds. Forty minutes later, they come to the theatre tent.

"This festival is **huge**!" says Mum. "It's one hour from **end** to end!"

The Black and Red Theatre group enter the stage.

"We don't like this theatre tent," says Charlie, after some minutes. "It's for parents. Can we buy some ice creams?"

"Yes," says Mum. "Here's ten pounds. Please come back and find us."

Charlie and Katy walk through the crowds and find a stall near the Pyramid Stage. They buy ice creams and go back to the theatre tent. But the stage is empty now, and they cannot see Mum and Dad.

WHERE ARE MUM AND DAD?

"Where are they?" says Charlie.

"Maybe Mum and Dad are looking for us too," says Katy.

Katy and Charlie walk through the crowds of people.

"Where are we?" says Katy. "I don't know this area. There are many hills here – which hill is our tent on? Maybe Mum and Dad went back there."

"Wait!" says Katy. "Listen. Can you hear music?"

"Yes!" says Charlie. "Is it . . .?"

WHERE ARE MUM AND DAD?

"It's Adriana Perez!" says Katy.

"Yes, but it's coming from a speaker!" says Charlie. He laughs. "She's singing 'Summer Song'."

Charlie and Katy see a crowd of young people around a speaker. Some of them are singing and others are dancing.

"Let's sing and dance with them," says Katy.

Charlie and Katy go and stand next to the speaker. Katy begins to sing, and Charlie starts dancing.

The children stop and watch them. "Wow! You two are very good," one of them says.

"Thanks!" says Charlie. "We love this song."

WHERE ARE MUM AND DAD?

"You're very good! Good at dancing *and* at singing. You're wonderful! *And* you're wearing my T-shirts!"

Katy and Charlie stop singing and dancing. A young woman is watching them. She has four people behind her.

One of the children stops the music.

"Are you . . . are you *Adriana Perez*?" says Charlie.

"That's me!" The woman smiles and takes off her dark glasses. Then she puts them back on quickly. "But don't tell the crowds!" she says, and laughs.

WHERE ARE MUM AND DAD?

CHAPTER FOUR
Summer Song

All the children's mouths are open.

"These are my dancers," says Adriana Perez. "This is Toria, Pete, Kenji and Jo."

"Hello. Please don't stop singing and dancing," says Toria. "You two are great."

"I can't sing in front of Adriana!" says Katy. "I'm too **frightened**."

"Me too!" says Charlie.

"Don't be frightened," says Adriana Perez. "Please dance and sing for us."

"Well, OK," says Katy.

The music starts again, and Katy begins singing "Summer Song". Charlie dances next to her. Adriana Perez and her dancers **cheer**.

SUMMER SONG

"You're great!" Kenji says.

"Yes, you must enter *Britain's Talent Contest*," says Adriana.

"Please can I have your autograph, Adriana?" says one of the children. She has a festival programme in her hand.

"Of course," says Adriana. "What's your name?"

Adriana writes her name on the programme and then takes some cards from her bag. She writes her name for Katy and Charlie and all the children.

"We must go now," says Adriana. "I'm the headlining artist this evening. Goodbye and enjoy Glastonbury. We hope to see you in the crowd tonight!"

"Katy! Charlie!" shout Mum and Dad. "There you are!"

SUMMER SONG

CHAPTER FIVE
On the Pyramid Stage

It is nine o'clock at night, and the family are at the Pyramid Stage. Katy and Charlie are very excited.

"Can we go close to the stage?" they ask.

"OK," says Mum, "but meet us at the Cornwall Fish and Chips stall at the end." She points to one of the food stalls.

"Cornwall Fish and Chips," says Katy and smiles. "OK!"

Katy and Charlie walk and walk through the crowds. It is very difficult, but now they are standing in front of the stage!

"Wow, this is great!" says Charlie. "We can see everything!"

There is lots of shouting and **cheers**. Adriana Perez is on the stage with her dancers.

"Hello, Glastonbury!" shouts Adriana.

She begins playing a song. There are cheers, and the crowd sing with her.

ON THE PYRAMID STAGE

Adriana Perez plays all Katy and Charlie's favourite songs. It is a great evening.

"Look, Adriana is waving at us!" shouts Katy.

She is right. Adriana is smiling and waving.

"This next song is 'Summer Song'," she says. "Charlie and Katy, can you come up on stage and help me with it?"

ON THE PYRAMID STAGE

"Yes!" shout Charlie and Katy together. The festival workers help the two children on to the stage. Charlie and Katy look at the huge crowd around them.

"Don't be frightened," says Adriana Perez, quietly. "You're wonderful."

Adriana starts playing her guitar and she sings "Summer Song". Katy sings with her. Charlie starts dancing. Then Adriana stops singing. Now the crowd can only hear Katy. They begin shouting and cheering.

ON THE PYRAMID STAGE

A FESTIVAL IN SUMMER

"Look at Katy and Charlie," says Dad. "They're on the stage with Adriana Perez!"

"They're our children!" shouts Mum to the crowd. "Our children are on the stage with Adriana Perez!"

"They have a lot of talent," says a woman next to her.

"Thank you!" says Mum.

Katy finishes "Summer Song", and Charlie **ends** his dance. The crowd cheer again.

"This is Katy and Charlie on the Pyramid Stage," says Adriana Perez. "Give them one more cheer!"

"What a *wonderful* night," thinks Katy.

CHAPTER SIX
Back home

It is Monday afternoon. The Mercers are home.

"I love Glastonbury!" says Charlie.

"I love it too," says Katy. "But I feel sad because it's ended."

"We can go again," says Mum. "I can enter for next year's tickets."

BACK HOME

It is Saturday evening, and the family are watching *Britain's Talent Contest*. Ezra Smith wins.

"They want people for next year's contest," says Dad. "Maybe you two can enter?"

Charlie looks at Katy. "Remember Adriana's words?" he says. "*You must enter Britain's Talent Contest.*"

"Yes, of course we must enter!" says Katy. "Oh, thank you, Adriana Perez, and thank you, Glastonbury!"

During-reading questions

CHAPTER ONE
1. What are Charlie and Katy watching on TV?
2. "You enter every year, and you never get them," says Charlie. Why does Charlie's mum never get tickets?
3. What artists are going to Glastonbury this year?

CHAPTER TWO
1. What can the family see from their tent?
2. What do the family do at the festival that evening?

CHAPTER THREE
1. How do Katy and Charlie feel about the theatre tent?
2. What music do Katy and Charlie hear?
3. Who is the woman in the dark glasses?

CHAPTER FOUR
1. What do Katy and Charlie do for Adriana Perez?
2. Does Adriana like their singing and dancing? What does she say to them about it?

CHAPTER FIVE
1. Where do Katy and Charlie stand?
2. Why do the crowds begin shouting and cheering to "Summer Song"?

CHAPTER SIX
1. Who wins *Britain's Talent Contest*?
2. Why do Katy and Charlie get excited?

After-reading questions

1 What are the names of the Glastonbury stages in the story?
2 What artists do the family watch?
3 Why does Katy say, " . . . thank you, Glastonbury!", do you think?

Exercises

CHAPTER ONE

1 Match the correct word to the meaning in your notebook.
Example: *1 – c*

1 enter	a very good
2 laugh	b to play at the end of an evening's music festival
3 shout	c to go into a place or thing
4 line-up	d to speak when you are excited or angry
5 headline	e We do this at funny things.
6 wonderful	f people who play at a music festival

CHAPTER TWO

2 **Write the correct word in your notebook to complete these sentences.**
1. The festival is ***between*** / **under** many big green hills.
2. There are quiet areas and **dance** / **swimming** areas.
3. There are hundreds of **pizza** / **food** stalls.
4. Charlie is a **cat** / **bird** and Katy is a **cat** / **bird**.
5. The family **watch** / **sing** Jackie Olson.
6. They **sing** / **dance** to all her songs.

CHAPTER THREE

3 **Are these sentences *true* or *false*?**
1. Charlie and Katy are wearing their Adriana Perez T-shirts because they are cold. *false*
2. The Black and Red Theatre Group are at the theatre field at 1 p.m.
3. The festival is small.
4. Charlie and Katy buy ice creams near the Pyramid Stage.
5. Some young people are watching Adriana Perez on stage.
6. The woman in the dark glasses is Adriana Perez.

CHAPTER FOUR

4 Contract the verbs in your notebook.
1. do not _don't_
2. can not
3. I am
4. you are
5. what is

CHAPTER FIVE

5 Match the two sentences, or parts of sentences, in your notebook. Example: *1 – d*

1. It is nine o'clock at night,
2. "Wow, this is great!" says Charlie.
3. "Charlie and Katy,
4. Adriana starts playing her guitar
5. "Our children are on the stage
6. "This is Katy and Charlie on the Pyramid Stage," says Adriana Perez.

a. "We can see everything!"
b. and she sings "Summer Song".
c. with Adriana Perez!"
d. and the family are at the Pyramid Stage.
e. "Give them one more cheer!"
f. can you come up on stage and help me with it?"

CHAPTER SIX

6 **Choose the correct verbs to complete these sentences in your notebook.**

	are	feel	love	go
		enter	says	

1 It is Monday afternoon. The Mercers ....*are*.... home.
2 "I .... Glastonbury!" says Charlie.
3 "I love it too," says Katy. "But I .... sad because it's ended."
4 "We can .... again," .... Mum. "I can .... for next year's tickets."

Project work

1 You are Katy. Write a diary page about Saturday at Glastonbury.

2 Plan a music festival in your country. Think about the artists, stages, theatre and food stalls. Draw a map of your festival and make a poster about it.

3 Write a newspaper report about Katy and Charlie's night on the Pyramid Stage.

4 Write the words to "Summer Song".

5 Who is your favourite singer? Make a presentation about him or her.

6 Katy and Charlie enter *Britain's Talent Contest*. Write the next chapter of the story.

An answer key for all questions and exercises can be found at **www.penguinreaders.co.uk**

Glossary

area (n.)
a part of a place

around (prep.)
in many parts of a place

café (n.)
a small (and often cheap) restaurant

cheer (v. and n.)
to *shout* because you like a person or thing. This is a *cheer*.

colourful (adj.)
If something has many different colours it is *colourful*.

crowd (n.)
a lot of people together in a place

end (n. and v.)
something finishes, or stops, at the *end*. It *ends*.

enter (v.)
to go into a place or thing. In this story, you *enter* your name because you want to be part of something (a *festival* or *talent contest*).

excited (adj.)
very happy because you are waiting for a good thing

festival (n.)
a big party with music, food, etc. in a *field*

field (n.)
a large green *area* with a fence (= a fence goes *around* a place; it can stop people or animals from going in or out). Cows and sheep usually live in *fields*.

frightened (adj.)
People are *frightened* of bad things.

headline (v.)
to play at the *end* of an evening's music *line-up*

hill (n.)
You can see a lot of things from the top of a *hill*.

huge (adj.)
very big

laugh (v.)
We smile and *laugh* at funny things.

line-up (n.)
People play music at a *festival*. These people are the *line-up*.

quiet (adj.)
People do not talk a lot or *shout* in a *quiet* place.

shout (v.)
to speak when you are *excited* or angry

tablet (n.)
a small computer

talent contest (n.)
People dance, sing or play music because they want to *win* a *talent contest*.

tent (n.)
You put a *tent* in a *field*. You can sleep in it.

thousands (n. pl.)
many *thousands*. One *thousand* =1,000.

through (prep.)
from one *end* to the other *end*

win (v.)
to be the first in a game

wonderful (adj.)
very good

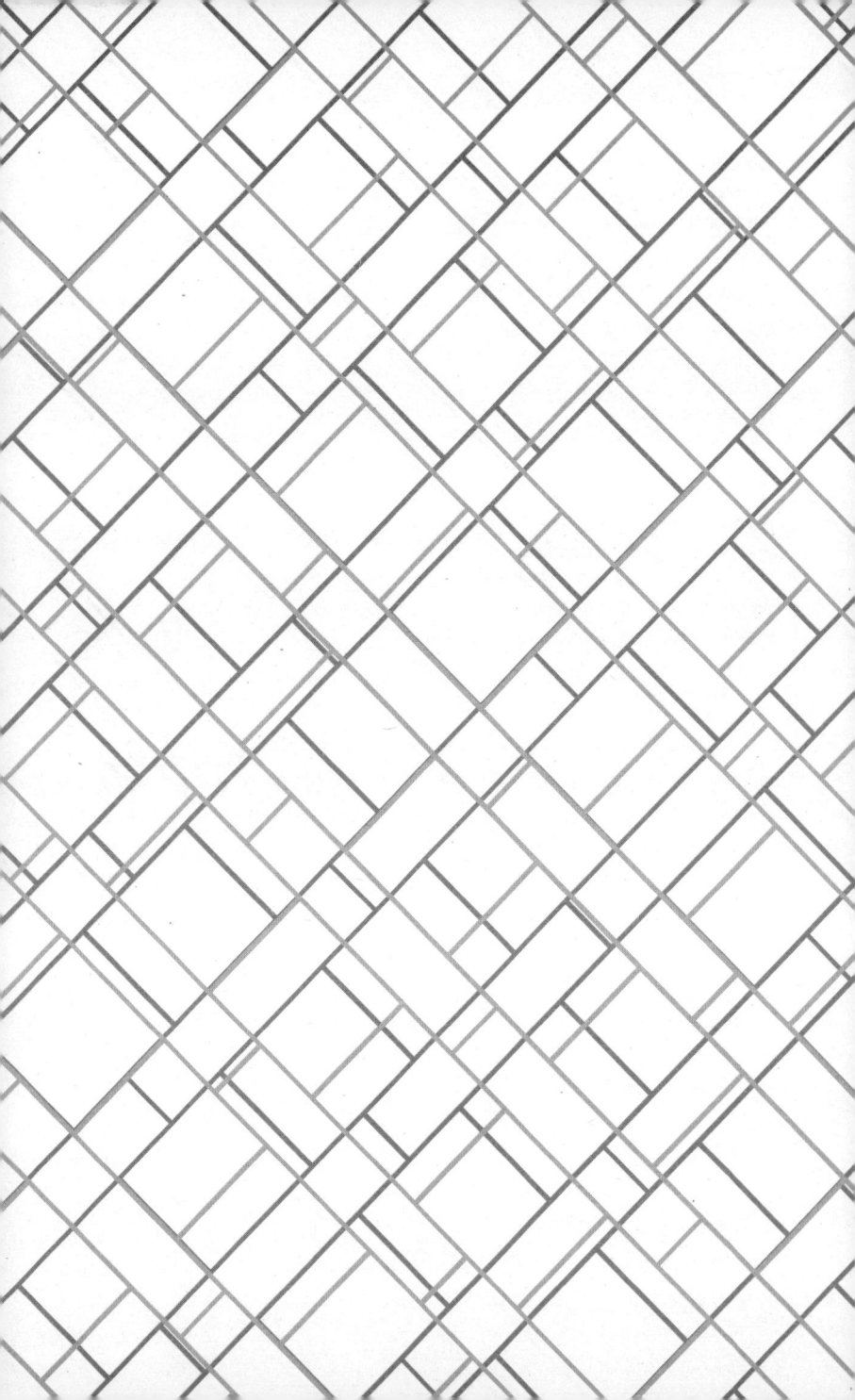